THE GOOD TIMES GAME BOOK

Douglas Kamstra, Compiler
Produced by the Young Calvinist Federation

BAKER BOOK HOUSE
Grand Rapids, Michigan

Contents

Getting Loose 3
Body Builders 12
Group-Talk Motivators 19
Make 'em Laugh 26
Games for the Great Outdoors 34
Special Times 38
Play It Like It Is 45

Introduction

Games are for fun, for recreation, for relaxation, for sharing good times, and for making new friends. But primarily games are intended for growing, for learning, and for discovering others and the Word of God.

All games must have a purpose. Merely playing a game to fill some time is self-defeating. When you begin to think about using a game, give some thought to *WHY* you want to use it. Ask yourself, "What do I want to achieve?" Once you answer that question you can begin searching for the best game to fit your purpose. Remember: choose a game to fit a purpose, not a purpose to suit a game.

With a little work, you'll be able to find a game to fit almost any purpose or goal you can think of. Here are a few goals you can achieve through games. With the proper game you can:

1. transmit and build unity in a group (p. 12).
2. release the tension present when "strangers" meet for the first time (p. 3).
3. start a discussion (p. 19).
4. illustrate what is happening "out there" in the real world and prepare individuals to meet those challenges (p. 45).
5. just have a good fun time together either indoors or outdoors (p. 34).
6. get your point across more effectively than with a lecture or study exercise (p. 19).

This book contains a variety of games to fit a variety of purposes. Some games you can play just for fun or as warm-up exercises; other games need to be followed with discussion questions and sharing in order to be effective.

Whether you choose a game from this book or from any other resource, be sure you know *WHY* you are playing it.

Copyright 1977 by The Young Calvinist Federation
Box 7244, Grand Rapids, MI

Reprinted by Baker Book House Company

First printing, January 1981
Second printing, November 1981

ISBN: 0-8010-7705-2

Printed in the United States of America

Getting Loose

Crowd breakers, mixers, ice breakers, or whatever you call them, are special games designed with one purpose — to make a group of people feel more at ease with one another. They can be a leader's most effective tool during the first few meetings of the year and throughout the year. If you use the right crowd breaker you can transform a room full of strangers into a group of sociable people who are talking, moving around, and laughing. Once a group has loosened up by playing a game, they will relax and enjoy the meeting more and be eager to participate in a discussion.

Most crowd breakers are short, easy games that can be effective in just a few minutes. Use them often to get a meeting or activity started with a bang!

BIRTHDAY RACE

Give the members of the group about two minutes to arrange themselves in the order of their birthdays. Anyone out of order is out of the game. Try the game again using height, weight, shoe size, or whatever else you can think of.

TOILET PAPER PULL

This game can be used for any size group. If the group is very large, break up into smaller groups of six or less. Have the group sit in a circle. Hand the first person a roll of toilet paper and instruct the group to take off as many pieces as they think they are going to need. Tell them to take at least three. When everyone has as many pieces as they want, tell them they must now tell something about themselves for every tissue pulled off. For some this could mean 25 things.

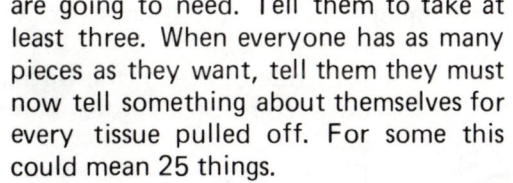

TOUCH IT

Divide the group into teams. Call out certain objects in the room like "light switch," "door-knob," or "window." Everyone must run over to that object, touch it, and then run back and line up their group in a single row. Do this for a number of different objects in the room. The winning team is the one who wins the most "heats." This game also works well outside.

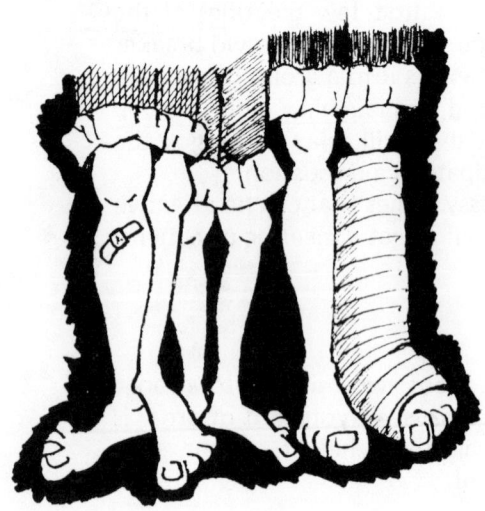

LEG LINE-UP

Have four or more guys roll their pants up to their knees. Then have the girls study the guys' legs and after a few minutes blindfold the girls. Shuffle the standing arrangement of the guys, and even substitute a girl in the line-up to make it more confusing. The girls must identify the guys by feeling their legs.

THINGS RELAY

Divide the group into relay teams and place them around the room. From the center, call out "things" you want a representative of the group to bring you. Award a point to a team each time they are first to bring you the article(s) requested. You'll want to tailor your list of "things" to your group but here are a few examples.

1. A picture of Abe or the Queen. (It's on a coin, but let them find that out.)
2. Five shoelaces tied end to end.
3. A boy with a ring on each finger of his right hand.
4. The name of each person in the group written down backwards.
5. A girl with six socks on her left foot.
6. A boy with four belts around his waist.
7. A girl carrying a boy piggy-back.
8. A girl wearing six shirts and/or sweaters.

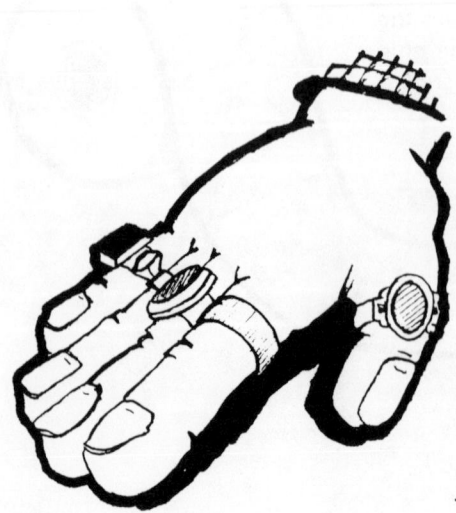

Be strict about accepting objects only in the manner requested. The team with the most points is the winner.

ACTION RELAY

Divide the group into two teams and line up in a row. At the opposite end of the room place a chair with a bag of instructions on it. Write the instructions on slips of paper and place them in the bag. Each team member runs to the chair, reaches in the bag, pulls out a slip with instructions, and goes through the directed action. He then must tag the chair before tagging the next person in line. First team completed wins. Some possible instructions are:

1. Run around the chair five times screaming continuously, "The British are coming, the British are coming!"
2. Run to the nearest bathroom, flush the toilet, and run back to the room.
3. Go get a drink of water.
4. Recite the poem "Mary Had A Little Lamb."
5. Go over to the other team and untie all their shoes.
6. Count how many pieces of jewelry the other team is wearing.
7. Go over to someone of the opposite sex on the other team and in a Dracula voice say, "I want to bite your neck."
8. Stand on one foot while holding the other in your hand. Tilt your head back and count, "10, 9, 8, 7, 6, 5, 4, 3, 2, 1, Blast Off!"
9. Run to the nearest person on the other team and scratch his head.
10. Run around the chair backwards five times while clapping your hands.

SIT ON 'EM

Place all the chairs in a circle, making sure that each chair has someone sitting on it. Then call off some items from the list below. Every person who "qualifies" must move one chair to the right. If someone already occupies the chair, they must sit on top of him/her. Use examples which apply best to your group. Here are some examples: "Move one chair to the right if you . . ."

— didn't use deodorant today
— are under 15
— drive your own car
— kiss with your eyes open
— have worn white socks in the last week
— dated a real loser last week
— didn't take a bath or shower today
— kiss sloppy
— didn't use mouthwash
— have green on
— have an outie belly-button
— believe in making-out on the first date
— think you are good looking
— have never been kissed
— have cheated at this game

BODY BUILDERS

Divide into small groups of about three people and have each group think of a machine, toy, appliance, or object in the home. They then must act out or imitate that object for the group. Some suggestions: a crackling fireplace, a washing machine, a stereo, a garbage disposal. Pick the winning group by popular vote.

LAWYER

Have the leader stand in the center of the circle (someone may also be selected from the group). He must go around the circle (in no particular order) and ask the players any sort of question he wishes. No player may answer for himself, however. His lawyer does that. The person sitting on his right is his lawyer. The answer does not always have to be the truth. If the person in the middle suspects the lawyer is lying, he may challenge the lawyer. If the middle person is correct, he trades places with the lawyer. If he is wrong and the lawyer was telling the truth, he must leave the game and the person to the right of the lawyer becomes "it." If the person questioned answers the question, rather than his lawyer, he too must leave the game. Last person in the game "wins."

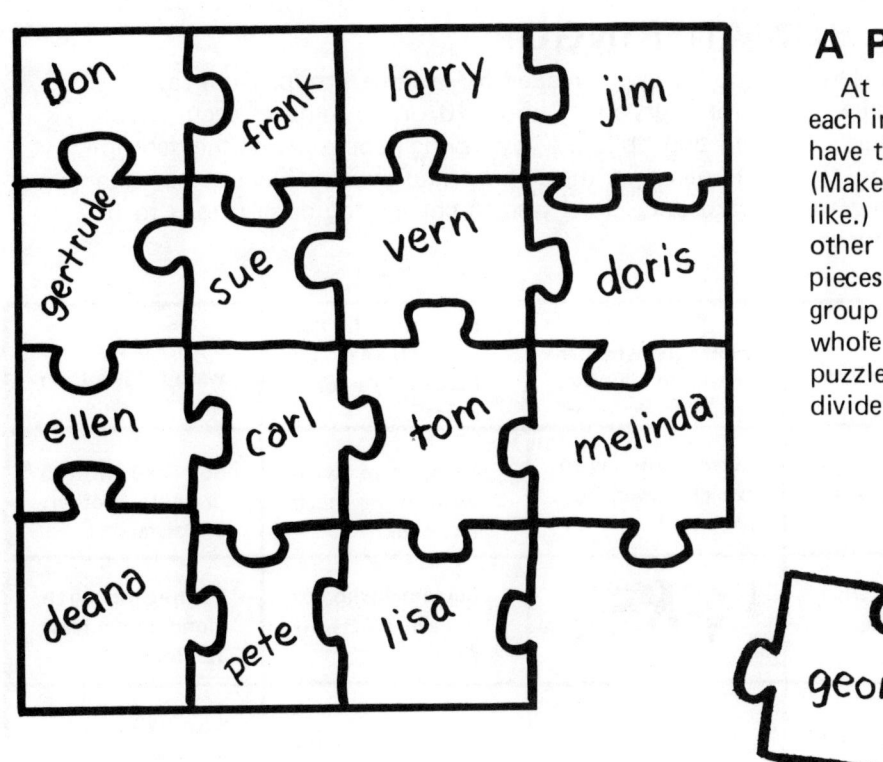

A PUZZLING EVENT

At the beginning of a meeting hand each individual a jig-saw puzzle piece and have them write their name on the back. (Make your own puzzle pieces if you like.) Instruct the group to find the other three or four individuals whose pieces connect to theirs. Finally, have the group arrange themselves to form the whole puzzle. By using several small puzzles you can use this activity to divide into small groups.

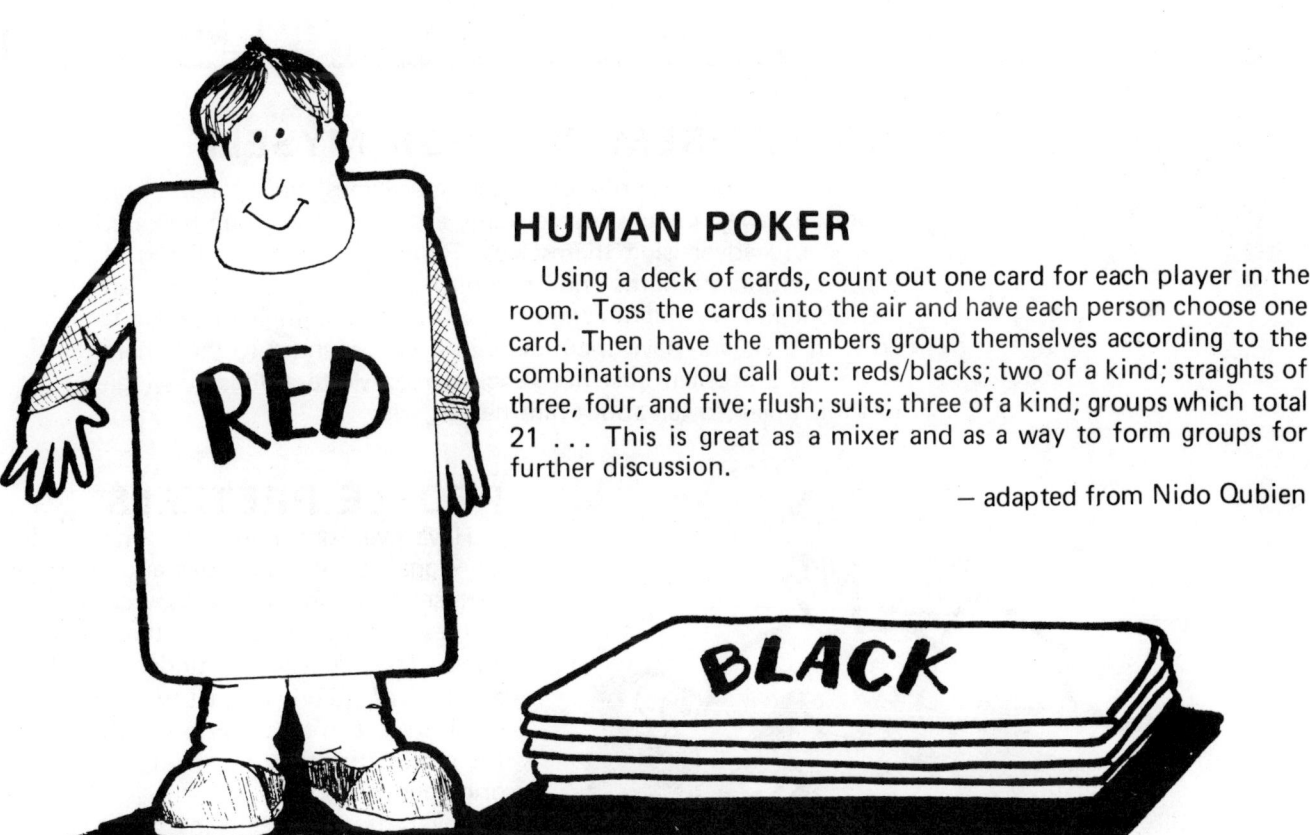

HUMAN POKER

Using a deck of cards, count out one card for each player in the room. Toss the cards into the air and have each person choose one card. Then have the members group themselves according to the combinations you call out: reds/blacks; two of a kind; straights of three, four, and five; flush; suits; three of a kind; groups which total 21 . . . This is great as a mixer and as a way to form groups for further discussion.

— adapted from Nido Qubien

HUMAN BINGO

Here's a good crowd breaker for a large group. Duplicate the chart below for everyone. Within 10 or 15 minutes each person must complete two "bingo's" by having people fitting the description sign their name in the appropriate square. Each person can only sign a card once. Feel free to change the descriptions to fit your group.

Someone who is going steady.	Someone with dyed or bleached hair.	Someone who has been to Europe.	Someone who has not been to McDonald's for a month.	Someone who wasn't kissed on their last date.
Someone with 10 or more cavities.	Someone with a birthday in February.	Someone who weighs over 200 pounds.	Someone who went to the beach last week.	Someone with 5 or more brothers and sisters.
Someone with perfect attendance in school.	Someone who owns their car — all of it.	FREE	Someone who has green in their shirt.	Someone with blond hair at least 12" long.
Someone who took a bath today.	Someone who got an A in PE.	Sign your own name.	Someone who writes poetry.	Someone who plays on the basketball team.
Someone who plays tennis.	Someone who has Fruit of the Loom underwear.	Someone who is wearing an ID bracelet.	Someone who is wearing red socks.	Someone who doesn't own a pet.

ADVERTISEMENTS FOR MYSELF

Gather a good supply of paper, magazines, newspapers, construction paper, pencils, paste, tape, etc. Have the group make up a brochure advertising themselves. Remind them that all ads always mention strengths and downplay any weaknesses if they are mentioned. They might even want to make up a jingle or slogan to go with their ad. Have them explain their brochure to the others. If time is a problem just have each person write a slogan or jingle or short poem to tell about him/herself.

PEOPLE PRETZELS

Have everyone join hands in a circle. On signal, they may move and entangle themselves in any way they wish as long as they don't let go of the other person's hand. They may crawl under, lift their hands over, step over; just twist and turn until they can't go anymore. Then tell the group that they must return to their original position.

A variation of this game is to select a committee (two or three) who leave the room while the others entangle themselves. When they return, it's their responsibility to reconstruct the circle.

NAME-O

This game works best with 25 or more people. Give each person a 4 x 6 card and a pencil. Have them divide the card into twenty-five sections, five squares by five squares. In the center they may put their own name. Then as quickly as possible they must ask other people to sign their names in the other blank spaces. Give a small prize to the one who has all the squares filled in first.

When everyone's card is full, have all the players take a seat. The leader will then point to the first person on his right, who must stand, give his name so that everyone can hear it, and then point to another person before being seated. Whenever a person introduces himself in this manner, all players may put a cross over that name if it appears on their card. Continue the introductions until someone has three "x's" in a row, then he cries, "Name-O!" If anyone calls out "BINGO" they are disqualified. First winner should get a small prize.

— Cora Hofstee

TELLING A YARN

Have the group sit in a circle. Hand a ball of yarn to someone who must give his name, tell something about himself, and then toss the ball to another person while still holding on to the end. This second person repeats the process and throws the ball to a third person. Soon a web of yarn will fill the circle. When a person is thrown the ball for a second time he must again state his name, the first thing he said about himself and add one other thing. Make sure everyone has had a chance before throwing the ball to a person a second time.

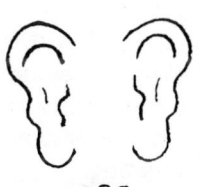

THIS IS YOU

Give each person a piece of paper and a pencil and have him draw the shape of his face on it. At a given signal, have group members ask other people in the room to draw the various parts listed below on his face shape. After a person has drawn a part, he must sign his name with his contribution. You may not have one person do more than one feature.

Nose _____
Eyes _____
Mouth _____
Eyebrows _____
Ears _____
Teeth _____
Hair _____
Something Creative _____

— Janet Postma

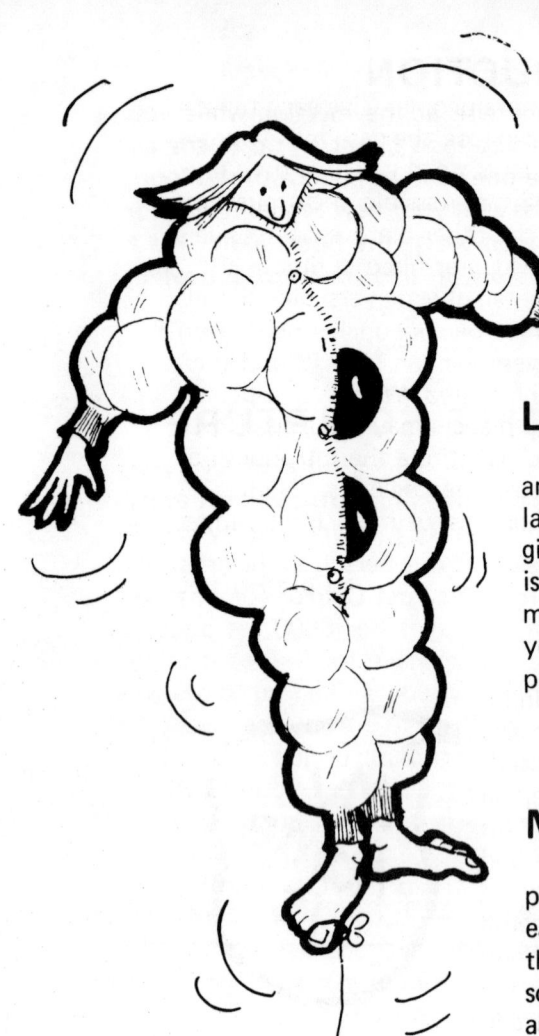

LONG JOHNS AND BALLOONS

Divide into two groups. Choose two girls of about the same size and ask them to come to the front. Have the girls put on an extra large pair of long johns (top and bottom) over their clothes. Now give each group a good supply of balloons. The object of the game is to have the team members blow up the balloons and see how many they can stuff inside the long johns in three minutes. After yelling "stop," count the number of balloons for each team by popping them while they are still inside the long johns.

MIXER IN MOTION

Before the meeting make out cards with instructions such as: pat my head, rub my belly, shake my hand, tickle my nose. Give each participant a card and instruct them to find the others in their group by following the printed instructions. That is, go up to someone and actually tickle their nose or whatever. This is a fun and hilarious way to divide a group.

CLOTHESPIN MIXER

Give everyone three to six clothespins. Then tell them that the object of the game is to get rid of their clothespins without having anyone else pin *THEIR* clothespins on them. Since everybody is trying to get rid of their clothespins at the same time as fast as possible, you'll have a rowdy and fun way to start a meeting.

PAIRS

Have everyone pair off and then give them a discussion question such as "What's the funniest thing that happened to you all week?" Cut the discussion short and let them pair off again to discuss another question. This question could be on current events or about school. Mix funny questions with serious questions about spiritual growth. This mixer is great for getting a group to settle down and to get them focused on program activities.

BALLOON INTRODUCTION

Introduce yourself to everyone else at the meeting while you keep an air (not helium) inflated balloon bouncing up in the air off your hand. You can only use one hand to bounce the balloon. Use the other hand to shake hands with your new acquaintance for ten seconds. Don't let your balloon touch the floor. Note: It's a good idea to have each person blow up their own balloon when they first walk into the meeting.

PEOPLE SCULPTURE

This game might not get everyone physically involved, but it will get everyone emotionally involved just by watching. Appoint one person as the artist and tell him "The First Church (or whatever church you like) has $500 set aside to have a statue made for the front of the church. They would like you to design a statue for them to portray teamwork (or laughter or strength or joy or harmony or whatever). Here are your lumps of clay to work with." (Choose three or four people to be the clay.)

Give the group about three minutes to work together to create the statue — it will probably produce a lot of laughs. Continue with more statues to get others in the group involved.

Body Builders

Many leaders think that by merely doing their homework, including a Bible study and being organized, they'll have a great group who is eager to open up, study God's word, and have heated discussions. But that's generally not the case because something very basic is lacking — a group feeling of togetherness.

No matter how hard a leader studies and prepares the lesson, if the members in the group don't know each other they won't willingly put themselves "out on a limb" by venturing their opinions. They must feel part of the group before they are willing to share; group building is very important.

The easiest and most enjoyable way of creating a "group" or a "team" is through games. Although the games in this section are specifically designed to help build a strong, cohesive group, they are not guaranteed to give you the "tightest" group around. They will, however, help to relieve the tensions which hinder your group from opening up.

The first way to create a team is to loosen up the group. Try some of the Getting Loose Games listed (p. 3) to get your group feeling more at ease with each other. Then move on to some of these other games to build up the group's "body."

WHERE DO YOU FIT?

Purpose:
1. To help the group understand and experience the significance of groups.
2. To help the group see that they are almost always members of some group, and that they belong to some groups even without their own consent.
3. To show the group that sometimes people enjoy the groups they are in, sometimes they have negative reactions to groups.

Method:
1. Get the entire group together.
2. Tell them that you will call out pairs of group labels, asking those who fit one description to move to one side of the room and those who fit the other to go to the other side.
3. Tell them to move to one side or the other as fast as possible.
4. Encourage them to be conscious of their feelings while they are participating.
5. Use some of the following groups but feel free to add your own. Notice the progression from very easy groupings to more difficult ones.

Groups which are very simple:
   boys/girls
   students from one school/students from another
   high school students/college students
   upperclassmen/underclassmen
   brown eyes/other color eyes

Groups which are a little more difficult and controversial:
- rich/poor
- concerned/unconcerned
- beautiful/ugly
- cool/uptight
- silly/serious

Groups which cause a great deal of difficulty in choosing:
- good/bad
- honest/dishonest
- those who like themselves/those who dislike themselves
- true believers/doubters
- pure/impure

Discussion:
1. Encourage members to discuss their feelings and reactions.
2. Try to draw out some of their new understandings about groups.
3. Explore the significance of the group they are members of. What does this mean about them as people? E.g., what is the relationship between being in the youth group and being in any other group?
4. Relate your findings to evangelism. What difference will it make if the person being reached is part of the Black group, worker group, elite group, etc.? Suggested Idea: Each group has its norms. If the "pitch" goes contrary to the norm of the group, your work will be more difficult than if it coordinates with the norms and thinking of the group.

COOPERATIVE SQUARES

Purpose:
1. To reveal the difficulty of cooperation without communication.
2. To reveal the effect of putting oneself first in a group setting.
3. To reveal the concept of synergy. One way of defining this concept is to say that people are displaying synergy when they are able to derive pleasure from the pleasure of other people.
4. To reveal the difficulty of giving to others.

Method:
1. Five squares of the same size and shape must be formed.
2. No member may speak or give any signals.
3. Members **may only give** cards to others.
4. No member may ask another for a card or signal how cards are to be placed.
5. A puzzle set consists of five envelopes containing pieces of stiff paper cut into patterns that will form 6 inch squares, as shown in the diagram. Cut the squares into parts and lightly pencil the letters "a" through "j" as shown below. Then mark the envelopes "A" through "E" and distribute the pieces as follows:

Envelope

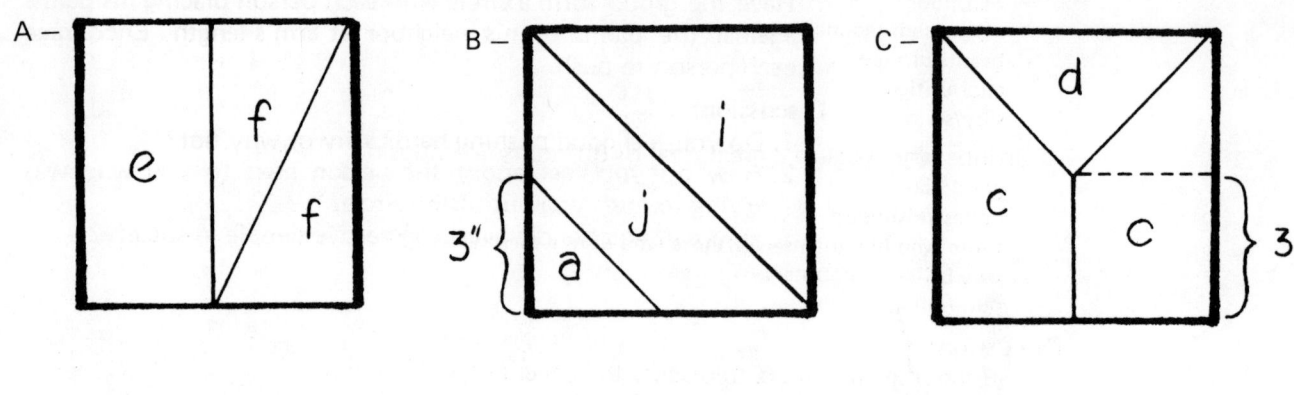

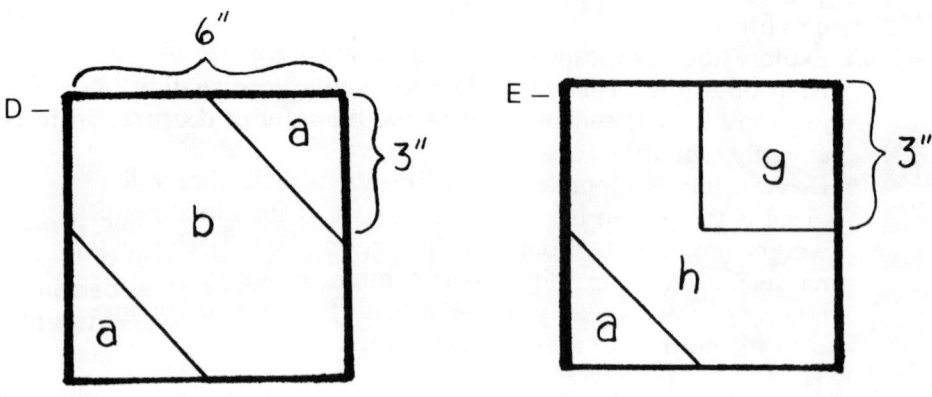

6. Erase from the pieces the small letters and write instead the envelope letters A through E, so that the pieces can be easily returned for reuse.
7. Several combinations of the pieces will form one or two squares, but only one combination will form five squares.
8. Make up a sheet for each participant including the purpose of the game and the questions so they can answer them individually.

Discussion:
1. Which members were able to adhere to the rules?
2. What rules were the most difficult for you to follow? Why?
3. What kind of feelings, tensions, and stresses did you experience?
4. Why do you think that some members had more difficulty in following the rules, making the squares, giving, etc.?
5. How did you feel about the person who finished last?
6. How much synergy was found in your group? How was it shown?
7. What did you learn about yourself through this experiment?

MOVING THE CIRCLE
Purpose:
To familiarize the members with the experience of aggression, a common element in group settings.

Method:
Have the group form a circle with each person placing his palms against the palms of his neighbor at arm's length. Encourage each person to push.

Discussion:
1. Do you feel good pushing hard? Why or why not?
2. How do you feel about the person next to you who was trying to push you out of the circle?
3. How can you handle overly aggressive people in society?

SHOE TIE

Purpose:
1. To reveal the difficulty of cooperation.
2. To emphasize the necessity of cooperation to get something done.

Method:
Divide all the people into groups of three. Taking turns, have two people untie and then retie the laces of the group with one person using his left hand and the other person using his right hand. Put a time limit on it. See who works together best.

Discussion:
1. How did you feel trying to tie the shoe using only one hand?
2. Did one of you start giving out commands?
3. Did you feel frustrated?
4. How did you resolve the problems you encountered?

PUT IT ALL TOGETHER

Purpose:
To show the group the need for cooperation as a group. (To show the Body of Christ concept in action.)

Method:
Have enough jigsaw puzzles on hand to provide one for every five or six people. The puzzles should be no larger than two hundred pieces. After everyone has worked on one puzzle for a while, they can rotate to another table and help out there. This may take two or three hours — depending on the puzzles — but will give your group an opportunity to get close in a relaxed, informal way. Another possibility is to get hold of one large puzzle (500 pieces). The entire group could work on putting it together.

Discussion:
1. What did you learn from this experience?
2. Did you understand what you were doing or did you just work on the puzzle?
3. How can we practically apply this concept of cooperation to our group? — to planning a party, etc.?

BLIND WALK

Purpose:
To encourage faith and dependence on group members.

Method:
1. Ask members to choose a partner.
2. One person must become leader, the other a follower; halfway they switch.
3. The follower should keep his eyes closed under all circumstances.
4. The leader then takes his companion for a walk either inside or out.
5. The leader has numerous options:
   a. He can attempt to describe the environment.
   b. He can remain silent.
   c. He can lead the follower through easy or difficult places.
   d. He can lead the follower into trees, people, etc.
   e. He can exercise whatever ingenuity is his.

Discussion:
1. Try to learn who could trust his leader and who could not.
2. Try to learn which people were trusted and which weren't.
3. Get them to see the importance of trust for their work as members of the Church of Christ.

FALLING AROUND IN A CIRCLE

Purpose:
To encourage faith and dependence on other members.

Method:
The group forms a small circle, with one in the center. The center person closes his eyes and falls in any direction. The group members catch him and pass him around the group. Each member takes a turn in the middle.

Discussion Suggestions:
1. Who did you trust in falling? Who didn't you trust?
2. Did you ever fear that the group would "gang up" and let you fall?

ALTER-EGO INTRODUCTION

Purpose:
1. To get to know one other group member.
2. To try to observe accurately as many things as possible about the other member.

Method:
1. Have the group divide into pairs.
2. Give each pair ten minutes to talk with one another; they should focus on three aspects of the other's being:
   a. How is his body feeling?
   b. What is he thinking?
   c. What emotion is he feeling?
3. In the larger group, each member introduces himself as the person he has been talking to, focusing the introduction on the three aspects discussed above.

Discussion Suggestions:
1. Discuss the reliability of making observations such as those required.
2. Discuss new insights gained from the experience.
3. Discuss the potential of such observation for witnessing. (You learn to see another person's condition. You learn how to approach others.)

TAKE MY ADVICE

Purpose:
To understand one another in order to get along better together.

Method:
Give each member a piece of paper and pencil. Have them write a paragraph or two on — "My advice to you on how to get along with me."

Discussion:
Encourage the group to stress their strengths but also to mention their weaknesses, pet peeves, and idiosyncrasies.

STRONG YET WEAK

Purpose:
To help understand and share someone's strengths and weaknesses in order to grow together.

Method:
Have each individual write down as many of his strengths as he can think of, but only 3 of his weaknesses. In the group share and discuss each individual's response.

Discussion:
As a group evaluate the strengths and weaknesses of the group. For example: they might find that they have some very strong points and a few weak ones. They should also try to find how the group can strengthen or overcome the weaknesses to make one strong group.

Finally ask them how they feel they will be best able to use their strengths and how they can overcome the weaknesses. Help the group feel united in their strengths and strong enough to overcome their weaknesses.

BALL TOSS

Purpose:
1. To produce feelings of frustration in the individual who is excluded.
2. To produce feelings of support and/or rejection in the group.

Method:
1. Select a strong, aggressive group member to be excluded.
2. Have the group form a circle.
3. Whisper to each group member that they must NOT throw the ball to the excluded person.
4. Tell the excluded person to play it cool, to hang loose.
5. Continue the exercise until it is obvious that he is excluded.

Discussion and Suggestions:
1. Ask the excluded person how he feels and why.
2. Try to learn the reactions of the others — did some of them enjoy keeping the other guy out?
3. Try to help them see the harm of exclusion: try to point out how exclusion can occur on a team; encourage them to prevent it.

ALPHABETS

Purpose:
1. To involve the group in a work project.
2. To give the group a common goal for working together.
3. To build group spirit.

Method:
Split the group into two or more teams. Supply each team member with a letter of the alphabet, making sure that each team has the same set of letters. Also include a few "blanks" for letters which they do not have. The members of the group must now spell out the answers, without talking, to questions given to them by the leader. First team to finish "writing" the answer gets one point for each letter in the work. Use Bible questions, funny questions, or anything you can think of.

Discussion:
1. Did you feel the urge to talk?
2. Did this project build the group cohesiveness? How?
3. Did you become frustrated with slow team members? How did you resolve this?

Group-Talk Motivators

Although no one has ever said it before, it must certainly be true that when two or three are gathered together there's bound to be a discussion: about the weather, about work, about school, about people, or about money. But sometimes a worthwhile discussion on the Bible or contemporary problems needs a little push to get going. Occasionally giving a lecture or reading an article will sufficiently stimulate the group, but sometimes they don't work. When that happens, try a game to get the group talking.

This section contains a variety of games designed for the purpose of starting a discussion. Sure, they're fun, but they're also very useful in getting your group to THINK and talk!

ROAD SIGNS

Make a program around road signs. Draw the signs before your meeting. Some good ones are: detour, slow, school zone, construction ahead, rough pavement, winding road, rest area. You could even save yourself some work and have your group make the signs as a project.

Before the meeting starts, hang the signs up in the meeting room. Tell the individuals in your group to go stand under the sign that most typifies where they are in life right now. Then have them discuss with the others in their group who have gathered under the same sign, why they chose that particular sign. Next, have the individuals go to their second choice and repeat the discussion. Finally have the group go to the sign that is least typical of their life right now.

Note: Leaders should provide scripture passages or reflection questions at each sign to help the group's discussion.

PASS THE BODY

Have about 10 or 12 people remove their shoes and sit in a circle with their legs and arms stretched out toward the center. Then ask for a volunteer to stand in the center with his arms crossed on his chest and his body rigid. He then must fall (keeping his body in a fixed position) toward the people seated on the floor. The players pass the "body" around and across the circle by pushing him with their outstretched arms. Obviously the person in the middle must trust each member of the group to keep him from falling.

This is a good introduction for a discussion on trusting the Lord.

WHO'S GONNA GET IN?

Present your group with this situation: "The ocean liner you are on is sinking. Somehow you manage to get in the last lifeboat which has space and food for six people. Ten people are clinging to the sides of the boat in the cold water and will freeze to death in 20 minutes. You must choose the five people to join you since they are too shocked and numb to argue. These are the survivors."

Now describe each survivor — age, occupation, value system, sex, etc. Tell the group that they know the backgrounds of all the people from traveling with them. Some examples would be: an unwed pregnant teenager, a retired Navy doctor and his wife who refuse to be separated, a black college student, a prominent politician with racist views, a famous artist who is a homosexual, and a well-known crusader for legalized abortion.

This is a good game for starting a discussion on values.

ACT IT, LIVE IT

This is an exercise that will get your group into the Scriptures and at the same time expose them to creative drama. Divide your group into smaller groups of three or four. Give each group a text of Scripture they can act out. (Parables are especially suitable for this.) Have them meet in their small groups for about five minutes and then rejoin the rest of the group. Each group acts out their particular text while the rest of the group attempts to guess the passage. For starting a discussion, center all of the assigned passages around a given theme.

WHY AND BECAUSE

This game produces some hilarious results. Give everyone in the group two 3 x 5 cards and a pencil. Ask everyone to write down a question that begins with "why" on the first card. Collect these. Then have everyone write the answer to their question on the second card, making sure the sentence starts with "because." Collect these. Now mix up the cards in each pile. Distribute one card from each pile to each member of the group. Have them first read the question card out loud, then the answer card and see what crazy comments you come up with. For initiating a discussion, tell the group to ask questions on a certain theme.

REVERSE SCAVENGER HUNT

Divide the group into teams and give each team 10 to 12 small but useful objects: a comb, 12 paper clips, a pen, an apple, a sponge, etc. Instruct the teams to go around the neighborhood, knock on doors, and give the objects to strangers, one at a time. Tell them to pay close attention to people's reactions and to be sure they have the recipient sign a form saying they received the object.

When they all return, discuss the practical implications of "It is better to give than to receive."

IT'S MORE THAN JUST TALK

Draw three simple geometric shapes on a piece of paper. Divide the group into pairs and give each pair a pencil and paper. Explain to the group that one member of the pair must look at the object and then describe it to his partner who must try to draw it.

Round #1 — Partners sit back to back. Partner No. 1 simply describes the object. He may not say what the object is, he may just describe it. Partner No. 2 then attempts to draw the object. When each group is finished, have them compare No. 2's drawing with the original.

Round #2 — Choose another object and tell the partners that this time they may face one another and Partner No. 1 may use his hands in describing the picture. Once again, Partner No. 2 draws what has been described. When finished, compare results.

Round #3 — Try still another object. This time partner No. 1 may face No. 2, use his hands, and answer questions. Partner No. 2 again draws a picture and then compares it with the original.

DISCUSSION: Communication is not just words, it also includes gestures and movements. Communication is a two-way process. Discuss frustration in communication. Imagine the world of the mute and deaf. Read Acts 1:8 and discuss the implication of this exercise for our Christian witness.

GOSSIP

Select a very short story or newsclip from the paper. Have everyone sit in a circle. Give the newsclip to the first person and have him read it to himself. He must then whisper the story to the person on his right. The story continues this way around the circle until the last person hears the story. He must then tell it out loud. Naturally, the story will be somewhat different.

There is a great deal of Scriptural material dealing with "Thou shalt not bear false witness against your neighbor," which should help you with a discussion on listening, gossiping, and rumors.

VALUE AUCTION

Give everyone in the group $10,000. Tell them that they now have no value system but must "buy" the values they want through an auction. Before the game, write each value on a 3 x 5 card. Put its corresponding point on the back. Examples:

Fruit of the Spirit Values: patience, longsuffering, love, kindness, peace, etc. = 4 points.

Qualities or Values such as: industriousness, trustworthiness, honesty, reverence, etc. = 3 points.

Selfish Values: wealth, beauty, strength, intelligence, etc. = 2 points.

Material Things: boat, car, motorcycle, big home, color TV, etc. = 1 point.

Auction off each value. The players must bid on that value with their "play money." The value goes to the highest bidder. When all the value cards are auctioned off, have each person total the number of points printed on the back of each card he purchased.

Although the person with the most points wins the game, do not tell the group that before the game begins. After the game break up into discussion groups and talk about how important values are to the personality of a person, especially to a Christian.

WORLD HUNGER

This game works the best with about 100 people. It can also be adapted to multiples of 100, however; or with a little work, adapted for even a smaller group of 50 or so.

Divide the group at random (pick country names out of a hat) as follows:
— U.S. — 6 people (give them half of the food)
— Europe — 12 people (give them 20% of the food)
— Middle East — 3 people (give them 5% of the food)
— Asia — 30 people (give them 9% of the food)
— Africa — 24 people (give them 7% of the food)
— South America — 24 people (give them 9% of the food)

The random choice symbolizes the fact that no one can choose what country they're born in. Label one table for each group with the continent's name and have the "citizens" sit around it.

Tell the group that this is an experimental situation, and that people are divided proportionately according to the world population and amounts of food. Pass out the food (make it something that everyone would want to eat). Do not interfere if at all possible.

DISCUSSION: What happened? How did you feel? What is the Christian response or responsibility to this? (Isaiah 58:3-12; Matthew 25:31-46; and Luke 12:48 are very helpful.)

WHAT'S YOUR BAG

For this game each person will be required to bring a large grocery bag and several articles from home. The articles should represent aspects of your personality. For example, an alarm clock could be used to show that you are a punctual person or a bright-colored balloon to show that you are happy and carefree.

The articles should be placed in the grocery bag. Each person will present the contents of his/her bag to the group and explain why the items represent his/her personality. An interesting sideline is to put all of the bags together and have each person select one without knowing the contents. A great deal of imagination will be required to apply another person's selections to your personality. You may also want to try to guess the owner of each bag.

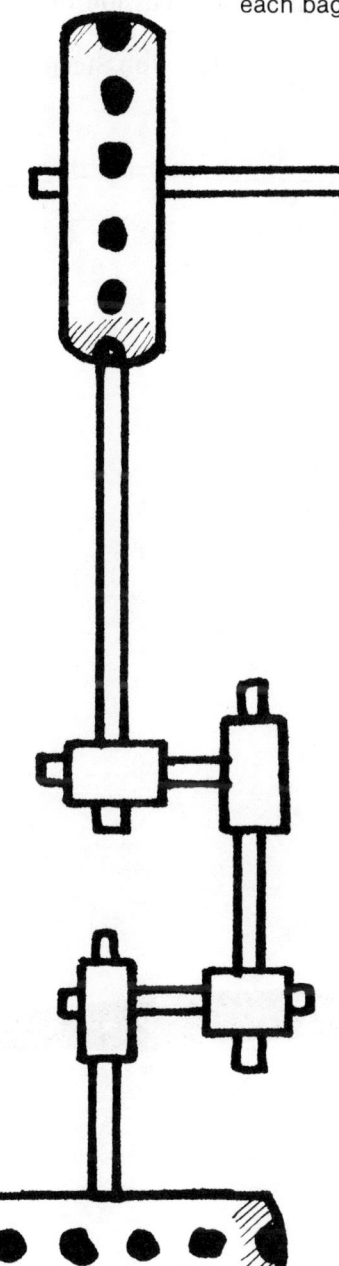

TINKER TOY TINKERING

Borrow several tinker toy sets. The more tinker toys the better. Make sure you have a variety of sizes and colors. Although this activity is a lot of fun, prepare your group to do some serious thinking and sharing.

Have each person construct a rather simple figure out of the tinker toys. Each part of the figure should represent a particular like or dislike. For example, someone's figure of a blue tinker with two small sticks coming off the side could mean that he likes cross country and track. Another figure attached to the blue one could represent his dislike for spinach. Each individual's structure should be pretty big with parts showing various likes, dislikes, animals, sports, his relationship to God, etc.

Put a time limit on how long each individual should "tinker." Then have one individual explain his structure to the rest of the group. The next person in line should then explain his creation. If these two share any likes or dislikes, the figure should be joined together at that point. Proceed this way until the entire group has made one construction. Through this "building" experience, the group should come to a better understanding of their neighbors and themselves.

— Steve Katerberg

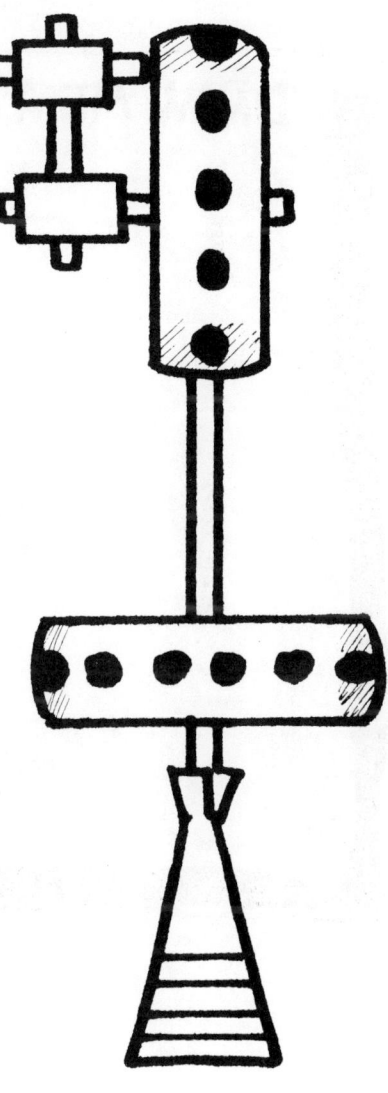

DRAW ME A PICTURE

Give each player a plain sheet of paper and a pencil and tell them they have about ten minutes to draw a detailed picture of anything they want. Have the group pair off and sit down back to back. One player of the partnership must *tell* the other person about his picture so that the other person can draw it. The drawer must not see the picture or ask questions. The person describing the picture can only use general language, like "a triangle, long line, short line, etc." After ten minutes reverse the roles.

Collect the papers, keeping the teams' drawings together. Then the group must decide which couple had the best "communication." The better the pictures, the better the communication.

For variety try grouping close friends or people who barely know each other. This game serves as a basis for a discussion on listening and expressing yourself clearly.

— Rev. Bob Steen

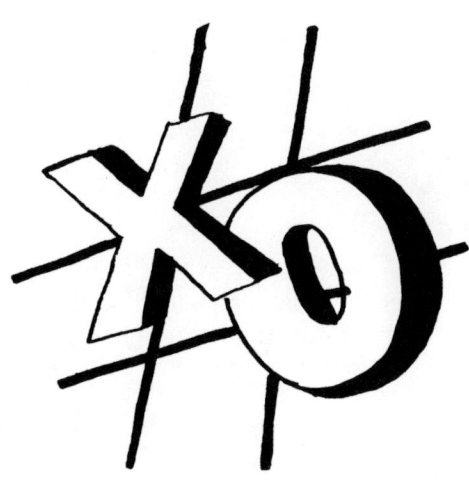

TIC-TAC-TOE

Set up nine chairs in the traditional format. Divide the group into two teams and have a set of prepared questions regarding your topic or theme ready. As each team member in turn correctly answers a question or makes a decision, they may take a seat on the "board." There must be no talking between team members. The game will be fun, and a little difficult because the players must all pay attention to who is on their team. If they talk or give the wrong answer they cannot score. The first team to win "X" number of games wins. Review and discuss the questions used during the game when you're through.

STARTING OVER

This game is very similar to "Who's Gonna Get In," but different enough that you could play both games.

Divide into small groups and present this situation: "The world is coming to an end. There is a cave big enough for only ten people to hide in. The ten are:

1. An accountant
2. His pregnant wife
3. A liberal arts co-ed
4. A pro-basketball player
5. An intelligent female movie star
6. A black medical student
7. A famous novelist
8. A bio-chemist
9. A 70-year-old Christian minister
10. An armed policeman

At the last moment a small earthquake occurs and there is only room for six people. As a group determine who is going to go in the cave and why."

Assign one person in each group to watch the process of working out the problem. How did the group solve the problem? Were there any conflicts? What caused them? Did your opinion get recognized or were you ignored? What was the criteria for deciding? Instead of looking at the actual people (not important in this game) look at the group process of give and take.

Make 'em Laugh

Everyone likes to have fun. Everyone loves to laugh. And what better way is there to laugh and have fun than through a game? Here are some games that are perfect for only one purpose — having a good time.

FARMER DRESS UP RELAY

Place long underwear, overalls or pants with suspenders, a bandanna, a wig, a shirt, a corn cob pipe, an old hat, etc. in a paper bag. On the signal to go, the first team members rush to the bag, put the clothes on top of their own, model them for the audience, take them off, put them back in the bag without ripping it, and finally run back to the line to tag the next person. Make sure each person is properly dressed, using *all* the clothes before they start modeling and undressing.

CRAZY CHARADES

Play this game the same as ordinary charades but add this twist. Each person must spell out the charade using his backside! Be prepared for a lot of laughs!

JAWS

Mark off "islands" on the floor with masking tape or chalk. Make them in a circular pattern around the room. Instruct the group to move around the circle to some music you've selected. (Use either a record or the piano.) When the music stops, everyone must move to the islands where they are safe. Those who can't squeeze onto an island can either drop out of the game, or become a "shark" who tags and "eliminates" people who fall off the islands. The leader should constantly decrease the size of the islands, eliminating some entirely so there is less space for the people. Participants may have one foot off the island as long as it is not touching the floor.

BEES

This is a rather rowdy activity and should take place in a large room without many natural hazards. Divide the group into two. For best results they should be mixed groups. Divide the room into three equal sections putting your groups behind imaginary or real lines on the outside thirds of the room. The center section becomes the playing area.

The rules for the game are rather simple. 1. You have to buzz like a bee — bzzzzzzzz — to enter the middle section. 2. All of the time that you are in the middle section you must maintain the buzzing sound. 3. If you fail to buzz while in the middle section, you are automatically disqualified. 4. The object of the game is to capture bees from the opposite team by maintaining your buzz and grabbing hold of the bees who dare venture into the combat zone. If a captured bee stops buzzing while you're in the combat zone he is disqualified. Those who are dragged to the other side by a buzzing bee are captives.

The game ends when all of the bees on one side are either captured or have quit buzzing in the center.

MIRRORS

Select two people and secretly tell them that one of them will be the leader and the other the mirror. The leader then performs a number of motions: patting his head, pointing to his nose, rubbing his eye, etc. The "mirror" duplicates the action at the same time. The group must then try to decide who is the leader and who is the "mirror." The winner is selected by the group. Continue choosing pairs until everyone has had a turn.

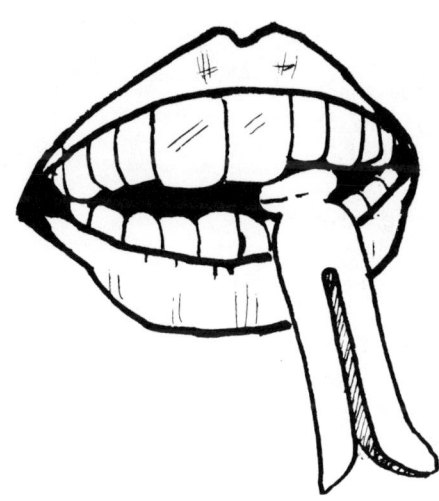

CLOTHESPIN RELAY

Divide the group into two relay teams. String a clothesline from one end of the room to the other, shoulder high to the average person. Clip 20 or more clothespins to the line. Have the teams line up on either side of the line. On the signal to go the first person in each team must run to the line, remove a clothespin with his teeth (no hands), and bring it back to the team. The first team done wins.

THE CONTAGIOUS GAME

Stand or seat the group in a circle so that everyone can see one another. The person on the end starts by describing his "ailment." For example, he might say, "My right eye twitches." Then everyone in the group must start twitching their right eye. The next person might say, "My left foot jumps" or "I have whooping cough," and everyone must start doing what he says. After a few people share their ailments, everyone should be jumping, twitching, coughing, sneezing, and having a great time. For double laughs, have someone take movies.

GUM SCULPTURE

Give everyone three sticks of chewing gum (use some different colors for variety), a 4 x 6 note card, and a toothpick. Let them chew their gum for *two* minutes only. Then tell them they must sculpture something with their gum, using the toothpick as a tool. The most creative sculpture made in a set amount of time wins.

SUCKER RELAY

Clear the room. Divide the group into two equal relay teams. Give each person a straw. The object of the game is to pick up a piece of paper (about 4" square) by sucking on the straw and carrying it around a goal and back. If a participant drops the paper, they must start over. Each person on the team must repeat the procedure. The first team finished wins.

BIRD, ANIMAL, FISH

Have everyone sit in a circle. Give the person who is "it" a club of rolled up newspaper. Tell him to call out the name of a person in the group and the word: bird, animal or fish. Ex. "Jim — bird." The person he has selected must name a bird, animal, or fish, whichever was called before "it" can count to ten. If he fails or gives an incorrect answer, "it" hits him on the leg with the roll of newspaper and he becomes "it."

SNACK RELAY

Instead of having the typical snack time, have a relay. Wrap up enough snacks for everyone in tinfoil and place an equal number in two bags. Vary the snacks as much as possible: cheese, marshmellows, crackers, apples, celery, carrots, cookies, cake, pickles, green pepper, a slice of onion, etc.

Divide the group into two teams. Each team member must reach into the bag, take out one item, and *eat it* before passing the bag to the next person on his team. Be sure that each person eats the item he selects! The first team to eat all of the items wins.

28

DROP THE TOWEL

Form a circle and appoint one person as "it." "It" walks around the outside of the circle with a towel and eventually drops it behind someone. As soon as he drops the towel behind a person, that person must run after "it." He must tag "it," before "it" can run around the circle and get into his spot. If he fails, he is "it." Otherwise "it" tries again.

FRUIT BASKET UPSET

Have the group sit on chairs in a circle. Then have each person select the name of a different vegetable or fruit. One person standing in the middle is "it." When "it" calls out two names, those two people must immediately change chairs while "it" tries to grab a chair for himself. The person left standing is "it." If "it" is unsuccessful in three attempts, he may call "Fruit Basket Upset" and everyone must get up and change chairs.

CLOTHES GRAB BAG

Take a variety of old clothes: hats, shoes, baggy pants, ties, dresses, etc. and put them in a large bag or pillowcase. Pass the bag around the group. Each person must select an article of clothing, put it on, and model it for the rest of the evening. The more clothes, the more fun.

Since some people will feel around in the bag until they find something they are "willing" to wear, try this variation: have each person pick a number out of a hat. They must then find and wear the piece of clothing that goes with the number.

BALLOON BASKETBALL

Divide the group into two teams and assign two people as referees. Arrange the chairs as shown below, with the rows nearest the end zone facing inward. Throw a round balloon into the middle. Each team must try to score by "passing" the balloon to their team members and into the end zone. Everyone must remain seated. If the balloon goes out of bounds the referee throws it back in. Each game consists of four periods with five minutes each.

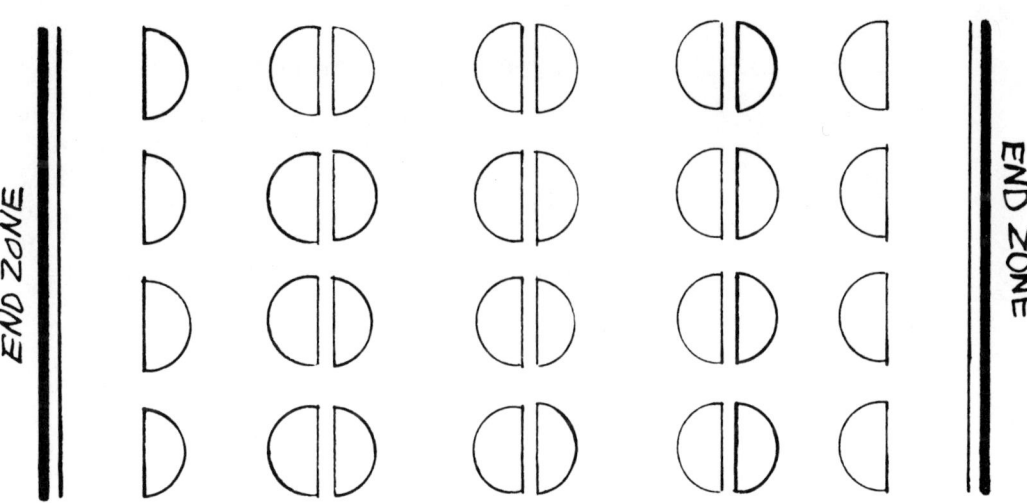

CHAIRS

DOG WANTS

Each person chooses a different animal name, and one person is "it." Someone in the circle begins by calling out his animal name with another animal's name: "Dog wants cat." The object is for "it" to swat the cat with some rolled up newspaper before the cat can call off another name. When someone is swatted before they can call off their own name and the name of another person's animal, they become "it."

BROOMSTICK HOCKEY

Instead of playing hockey with regular sticks and a puck use broomsticks and a baseball (rubber coated). This way everyone can play. No ice? Play it in a large room. Use standard hockey rules.

— adapted from a game in IDEAS

BUCKET AND WHISTLE

Line up two or more teams of five or six players. Give the first person in each line a small folding chair, an umbrella, and a bucket containing a whistle and a hat. At the starting signal the first player runs to the goal, unfolds the chair, sits on it, puts on the hat, raises the umbrella, and blows the whistle. Then he must put the hat and the whistle back in the bucket, fold the umbrella and the chair, and carry them all back to the next person in line, who must repeat the process. The first team to finish wins.

— Cora Hofstee

TIRE GRAND PRIX

Lay out a course around the church or other buildings close to your meeting place. Divide into a number of teams, about six to a team. Give each team a tire and set up the race like a relay. For a short course, change "drivers" each lap, for longer courses, a new "driver" may be needed at the half way point. For added excitement, allow "active drivers" to knock over, kick, or harass the other drivers.

SMACK

Everyone is seated in a circle with one empty chair in the center. Place a rolled up newspaper "club" on the center chair. The person who is "it" takes the club and strikes one of the seated players on the knee. "It" must put the "club" back on the chair and sit in the victim's seat before the victim can get up, run to the center chair, grab the "club" and smack "it." If he is successful, he retains his seat. If he is unsuccessful, he becomes "it." If the chair in the center is knocked over, the person responsible remains/becomes "it."

— adapted from Nido Qubein

PASS THE FEET BALL

For this activity you will need several balloons for each small group. Have the small groups (6-10) sit on the floor in a tight circle. The team must blow up their balloon, pass it around the group five times with their feet (no kicking, just passing by gripping it between their ankles) and have the last person pop the balloon by sitting on it. The first team done wins. If they break the balloon before they are done, they must start over. Have some extra balloons on hand.

— adapted from "Adventures with Youth"

SIZE TEN PLEASE

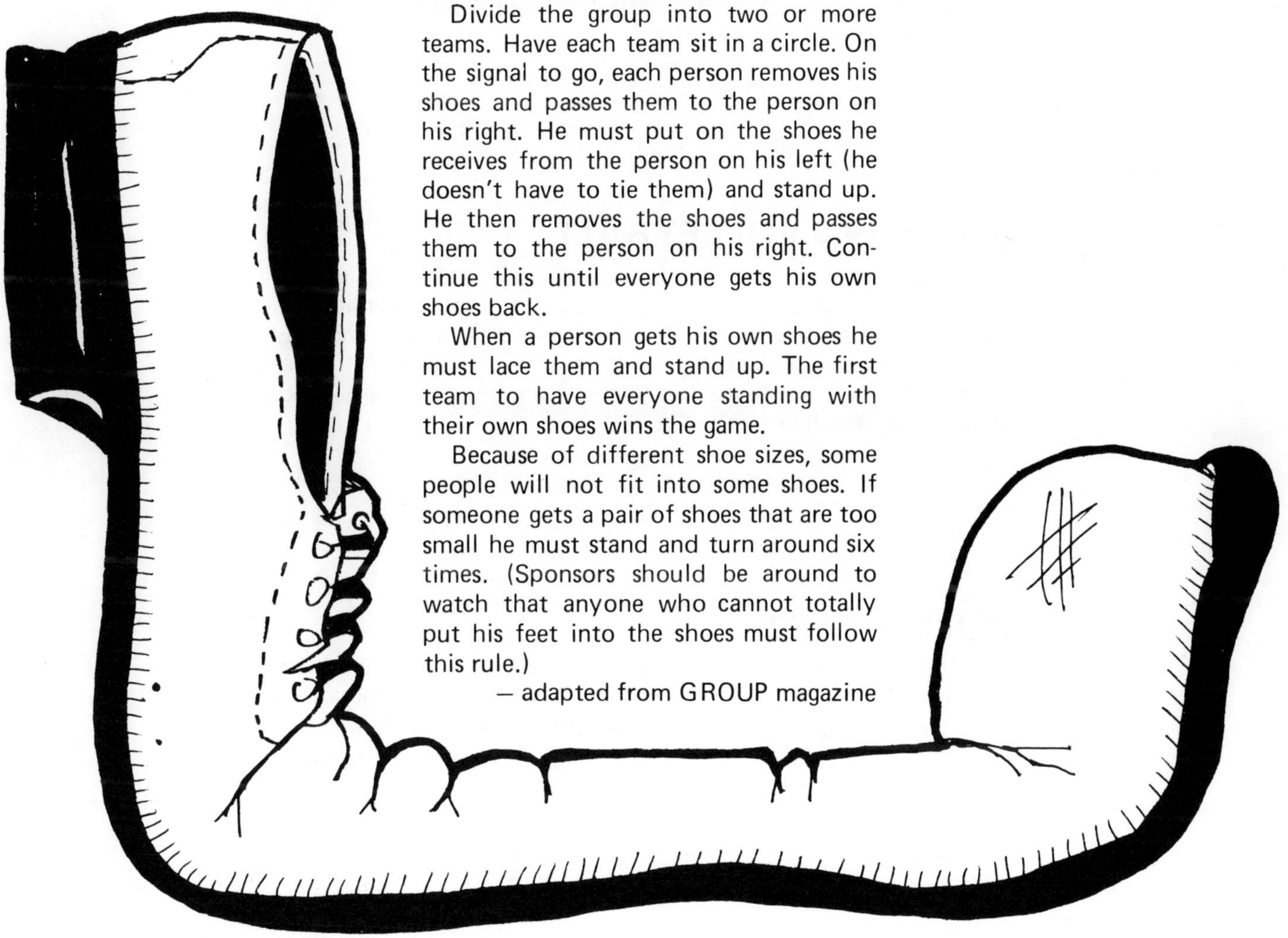

Divide the group into two or more teams. Have each team sit in a circle. On the signal to go, each person removes his shoes and passes them to the person on his right. He must put on the shoes he receives from the person on his left (he doesn't have to tie them) and stand up. He then removes the shoes and passes them to the person on his right. Continue this until everyone gets his own shoes back.

When a person gets his own shoes he must lace them and stand up. The first team to have everyone standing with their own shoes wins the game.

Because of different shoe sizes, some people will not fit into some shoes. If someone gets a pair of shoes that are too small he must stand and turn around six times. (Sponsors should be around to watch that anyone who cannot totally put his feet into the shoes must follow this rule.)

— adapted from GROUP magazine

NEWSPAPER NIGHT

Find a large gym or room and gather lots and lots of newspapers, garbage bags, and masking tape. Take a scale along, too. For preparation:

1. Ask everyone in the group to bring old papers from home.
2. Purchase several copies of the same newspaper a few days prior to the event.
3. Go through the paper you brought and choose several ads and articles.
4. Mark a line across the parking lot or use masking tape to mark a line on the gym floor. Wear your "grubbies" because newsprint is very dirty. When the group arrives, divide them into teams and give each team about 100 lbs. of newspaper. Make sure that each team has identical copies of the newspapers you brought somewhere in their stack.
5. Now include the following activities. In 3-5 minutes find out which team can:
   — crumple the most newspaper and throw it past a distance of about 20 feet.
   — be the first team to completely bury two people in crumpled newspaper.
   — make the highest pile in five minutes.
   — be the first team to find certain ads and articles you have chosen from the similar newspapers.
   — get all of their newspaper in a garbage bag first.

Add as many activities as you want. Give points for every activity and award a prize to the winners.

SIT DOWN VOLLEYBALL

Divide into two teams. Set up a volleyball net about five feet off the floor and get a beachball about the size of a volleyball. Have the teams sit cross-legged on either side of the net and play "volleyball" using volleyball rules except for the serve. All serves must come from the center of the group and must be overhanded. No one may use their feet.

PULL APART

All the guys sit on the floor and link arms and legs as tightly as they can. Then the girls try to pull the guys apart. Any tactics are fine. Tickling is great. There are no winners, but lots of fun.

— adapted from GROUP magazine

BUZZ

Have all the players sit in a circle. The first player starts counting with "1," the next player says "2," and so on around the circle. Whenever a player has a number divisible by or including the number seven, he must say "buzz" instead. Any player who makes a mistake is out of the game, and the game starts over with one. The last person in is the winner.

For added difficulty keep adding additional numbers and sounds. "Five" can be "brrr." When a number is divisible by both "5" and "7" both sounds must be used. This also applies for numbers like "57" or "75." If this becomes too easy, add "3."

PASS THE BODY

Have everyone lay down on the floor alternating the feet of one person with the head of the other. Have them pass each other over the top one at a time. You can divide into two teams for a relay race. The person being passed may not touch the floor, and those laying on the floor may only use their hands.

ROUND ROBIN

Have everyone stand in a circle around a ping-pong table. Place one ping-pong paddle and one ping-pong ball on each end of the table. The game begins with one person serving. After he serves, he must lay down his paddle and move to the right. The person next to him picks up the paddle to receive the return. This process goes on at both ends of the table. The person who makes an error is out for that round. The game becomes really good when only two or three people are left in.

For variation, play this game on a volleyball or tennis court.

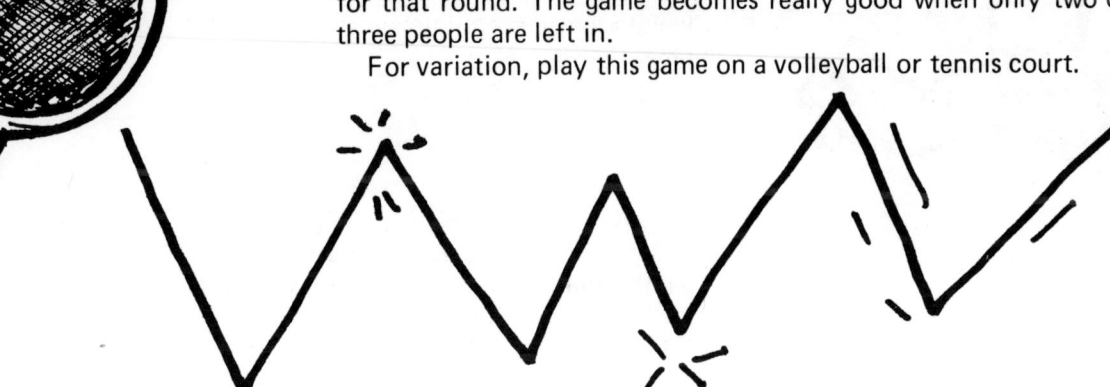

Games for the Great Outdoors

It's a beautiful afternoon or evening, you're on a retreat or on a camping trip, and you need to burn up some extra energy — so go outside in the open spaces and try one or more of these super outside game ideas.

TWO-BASE BASEBALL

The advantages of this game are that any number of people can play and very little equipment is required. All you need are a bat, a volleyball (or other large inflatable ball), two large bases ("Home" and "Away"), and an energetic group.

The bases should be set 60-120 feet apart, depending on the size of the group and the play area. As in conventional baseball each team gets three outs for every turn at bat. Outs result when the batter misses a pitch (only one strike per batter), when a fly ball is caught, when a runner is forced out at "Away," or when a runner is hit with the ball while not on base. The fielders may throw the ball at the runner.

In this game there are no foul balls. Any ball hit by the batter in any direction is playable.

A point is scored each time a runner crosses home plate. A runner at the "Away" base is not required to go home when a ball is hit. There is no limit to the number of runners allowed on the "Away" base at the same time.

PUM-PUM PULL-A-WAY

Mark off two goals about thirty to fifty yards apart. Then have all the players line up behind one goal area. Select one player as "it" and have him stand in the center of the playing area. When "it" calls out, "Pum-pum pull-a-way" all the players must run from one goal area to the other. After "it" tries to tag as many players as possible, everyone who is tagged also becomes "it." Then the leader calls the signal again. The last person caught wins.

WAR LOG

Suspend a six or seven inch diameter pipe or log between two trees four or five feet from the ground. One person straddles the log on each end and tries to knock the other person off with a pillow. Whoever touches the ground first or is knocked so that he is hanging upside down, loses. For safety, put a mattress, some straw, or blankets under the log.

FOUR CORNER TUG-OF-WAR

Play this game near a pond, stream, or lake. Get a heavy, long rope and tie the two ends together securely. Divide into four groups and give them each a corner. PULL! When one entire team is pulled into the water, they must let go of their corner. The game now becomes a three corner tug of war. When another team is in the water, the game becomes standard. The last dry team wins.

WELLS FARGO

Divide the group in half — one half are cowboys, the other half are Indians. Label a small part of the playing area as "The Bank" and fill five bags with "gold" (rocks) so that each weighs about fifteen pounds. Place a Band-Aid (labeled "C" or "I") on each person's forehead to represent their "scalp." At the beginning of the game give the cowboys the gold. Each team must try to get the most points. The cowboys receive ten points for every bag of gold they get to the bank; the Indians receive ten points for every bag that doesn't make it; both teams receive one point for every scalp they get. Once a cowboy or Indian is scalped they may not carry the gold. (Points are forfeited for violation.) Play for a predetermined period of time.

PIKE'S PEAK

Divide the group into two teams. Have them each choose a captain who stands at the top of a hill called "Pike's Peak." Give each team member a dixie cup, and each team captain a gallon jug. Put a water supply about 200-300 yards away from the hill. The object of the game is for the team members to fill their team captain's jug with water. The teams may try to stop each other any way they want, but boys may not attack girls. A five foot circle around the captain is a free zone. Anyone violating the rules must carry a full cup of water up the hill for the other team.

SCAT

Assign each person a number but include two extra "mystery" numbers. (If there are twenty-three in the group, count off to twenty-five.) While someone throws the ball into the air and calls a number, everyone must scatter. The person whose number was called must return quickly and try to catch the ball. As soon as he gets the ball he yells, "Stop!" He now takes three "giant" steps in any direction, before throwing the ball to hit someone. The person who is hit receives a letter, but if the thrower misses, he receives a letter. When someone receives four letters (S-C-A-T) he's out of the game. Whoever receives the letter must toss the ball next. If someone calls one of the unassigned mystery numbers, everyone receives a letter, but no one may use that mystery number again.

FRISBEE GAMES

Golf:

Set up a course of nine or eighteen targets. Targets may be trees, swing-set poles, fenceposts, or whatever else is available. The object is to hit the target with the frisbee in the least number of throws. The person with the lowest number of throws for the entire course is the winner.

Baseball:

This game is played the same as baseball except that a frisbee is used instead of the ball and bat. The pitcher throws the frisbee to the batter, who must catch it and throw it into the field. If the batter misses the frisbee, it is considered a strike. All the rules of conventional baseball apply to frisbee baseball. (If your group has a large number of inexperienced frisbee throwers, you will want to decrease the distance between bases.)

DUTCH SOCCER

Divide the group into two teams and place two pylons (or something similar) 150 feet apart to mark the goals. The object of the game is to knock over the pylons with the soccer ball. There are no boundaries, and all soccer rules apply. For more fun add another ball.

CAPTURE THE FLAG

The object of this game is simply to steal the other team's flag, but once the group starts planning strategies of "war," the game will become more challenging.

Divide the group into two teams. Assign each team half the available territory and carefully explain the boundaries. Give each team a flag to hide in some clearly visible area within their territory, and instruct them to mark one small area as their jail. Each player must have a handkerchief hanging from his belt. When one person grabs another person's handkerchief, the player must go to jail. He can be released only when another team member comes and "taps" him. The first team to capture the other team's flag wins.

SARDINES IN A CAN

Select one person to go and hide. After a few minutes everyone must start looking for him/her. Once they discover the person's hiding place, they remain hidden with him/her. The game lasts until everyone is hiding in the same place. It becomes increasingly hard to remain hidden as the group becomes larger and they begin to feel like "sardines in a can."

Special Times

Each year you're bound to have a party for a specific occasion or holiday. And at those special gatherings you usually feel obligated to play games especially designed for that particular occasion. Hopefully the following "special occasion" games will help you out.

CHRISTMAS

ALL I WANT FOR CHRISTMAS

Here's an easy game to help everyone at a meeting or a party remember each other's names. At the beginning of the meeting have everyone sit in a circle. The first person gives his name and an item he would like for Christmas that starts with the same letter as his name. E.g.: "My name is *Tim* and I would like a *train* for Christmas." (Of course the gifts don't have to be what you really want.) Each person in the circle must repeat the previous names and items and then add his own. By the time you go completely around the circle, everyone should be well acquainted.

CHRISTMAS CAROL PUZZLE

Take an old book of Christmas carols and cut up the old favorites into jig-saw puzzles. Make sure each piece has a few key words, or, if the group is more musically inclined, a few key notes. Pass out the pieces to the group. Have them find the other members of their sub-group by putting their Christmas carol puzzle together. When the groups are established, have them sing their song for the others.

MERRY MIXER

Give each person a card with one letter of "Merry Christmas" printed on it. Then have the group mix up and regroup with people who have the other letters needed to spell the phrase. The first group to have all the letters is the winner and screams, "Merry Christmas." This game will work best in a large group. Note: This game can be used for most holidays by just using the appropriate holiday greeting.

CAROLS IN HEADLINES

Here's a fun way to test how well everyone really knows the old Christmas songs. Copy the list of "headlines" making one copy for each person in the group. Include these directions at the top of the page: "Identify the following favorite Christmas songs. The clues appear in headline form."

HEADLINES

1. Baby Sleeps in Hay
2. Strangers Bring Gifts to New Child
3. Gift Necessary to Say Merry Christmas
4. Visions of a Blizzard
5. Fat Man Visits City
6. Wind Talks to Shepherds
7. All Is Quiet in Small Town
8. Angels Praise King
9. Request Made to Come to Bethlehem
10. Holly Used in Decorating
11. Deer Has Strange Nose
12. Group Sings and Laughs on Sleigh Ride
13. Group Gives Greetings for the Holidays
14. Nuts Cook in Fireplace
15. Happiness Comes to Earth
16. Man Created with Snow
17. Tree's Beauty Declared

CHRISTMAS SONGS

1. Away in a Manger
2. We Three Kings
3. All I Want for Christmas
4. I'm Dreaming of a White Christmas
5. Santa Claus is Coming to Town
6. Do You Hear What I Hear
7. Oh Little Town of Bethlehem
8. Hark, the Herald Angels Sing
9. Oh, Come All Ye Faithful
10. Deck the Halls
11. Rudolph the Red Nose Reindeer
12. Jingle Bells
13. We Wish You a Merry Christmas
14. Chestnuts Roasting on an Open Fire
15. Joy to the World
16. Frosty the Snowman
17. Oh, Christmas Tree

CHRISTMAS SCRAMBLE

Give everyone in the group a piece of paper and a pencil. Instruct the group to write Merry Christmas at the top of their paper. Then give them four minutes to write down as many words as possible using the letters in that holiday phrase. The person with the most words wins.

NAME THAT CAROL

Have the group pair off. Choose a wide variety of Christmas carols, hymns, and popular songs both old and new. Make up a hard clue to go with each song. E.g.: Give the name of the author or composer, give the name of the country where it originated (Germany for "Silent Night"), tell something vague about the lyrics (this song talks about snow for "Frosty the Snowman"), etc.

Give the clue, then have the pianist play the first three notes (melody only) of the tune. Be sure the music cannot be seen by the group. The first couple to raise their hands and correctly identify the tune gets five points. If they are incorrect they forfeit one point (this will discourage wild guessing) and the pianist plays the first four notes of the song. If someone guesses the tune correctly the second time, they receive three points. If they are incorrect, they too lose one point. Most everyone should be able to guess a song by hearing the first four notes, but play more if you think the song is particularly hard. After the song has been guessed, sing it entirely if you have all the music. The couple with the most points wins.

SANTA RELAY

Divide the group into two teams and have them line up. At a distance away from the groups, place two bags (one for each team) with the following contents: beard, hat, shirt and pants (red, if possible), a pillow case, a few toys, and a pair of boots. On the signal of "go" the first person must run to the bag, put on the beard and the clothes, stuff the toys in the pillow case, throw it over his shoulder and say in a deep Santa voice, "Ho, ho, ho, Merry Christmas." He must then take the toys out of the pillow case, undress, put everything back in the bag, and run back to tag the second person. The first team finished wins.

PIN THE NOSE ON RUDOLPH

Out of brown paper cut a large reindeer. Color it to look like Rudolph the Red Nose Reindeer, but leave off his large red nose. Hang it up. Give each person in the group a large red circle (a nose) with a pin through it. (Use tape if you don't have a "pinable" surface.) Line up. Blindfold the first person, spin him around a bit, point him in the direction of the reindeer. The person to pin or tape the nose on Rudolph the closest to where it belongs wins.

GIFT GRABBER

Exchanging gifts this Christmas? Then set a limit of how much to spend on each gift ($1.50) and tell the group to make the gift acceptable for either sex.

At the party place all the gifts in the center of the room. One by one, in clockwise fashion, have each person come forward to collect a gift (other than the one he brought). After everyone has a gift, deal out an entire deck of cards so that every person has an equal number of cards. From a second deck of cards, draw one card at a time and identify it out loud. Whoever has the corresponding card may exchange his gift for anyone else's until you use up the entire deck. The funniest part of the game comes when it's time to open the packages and everyone sees the absurd things that the others brought.

ONE-ARMED GIFT WRAP

This is a good crowd breaker. Have three couples come up to the front and give them some paper, tape, string, ribbon, a pair of scissors, and a box to wrap. Tell them they must wrap the package together but the boys may only use their left hands and the girls their right hands. Each must keep his other hand behind his back. Set a time limit. The couple with the best-wrapped package is the winner.

GIFT BY NUMBER

Have everyone bring a small, inexpensive novelty gift. Place all the gifts on the floor in the middle of the room. Pass around a hat filled with numbered slips and have everyone draw a number. The person with the lowest number chooses a gift first. The person with the next lowest number may either choose a gift already chosen or take one from the center. If he chooses someone else's gift, that person goes next; if he chooses a gift from the center of the room, the person with the next lowest number selects a present. No one may immediately reclaim a gift that was just taken from him. The process continues until everyone has a gift. Then open the gifts one at a time according to how popular they were.

PASS IT ON

Adapt this game (p. 27) for a Christmas party by using Christmas objects: a wreath, a candle, a tree ornament, a poinsettia plant, a log, etc.

NEW YEAR'S

SIGNED AND SEALED RESOLUTIONS
Have everyone write down their New Year's resolutions on a piece of paper. When everyone is done, hand each person an envelope and tell them to enclose the resolutions, seal the envelope, and address it to themselves. Collect the envelopes and mail them back in about six months, to let the group see if they kept their resolutions.

FATHER TIME RELAY
Adapt the game "Santa Relay" (p. 41) for a New Year's party by using the character of Father Time instead of Santa. In the bag place a cane, an hourglass (an egg timer is great), a beard, a sheet to wrap around, and a pair of glasses. Have each person say, "Oh dear, time's running out" as they look at the hourglass.

VALENTINE'S DAY

DARLING, IF YOU LOVE ME
Have everyone sit in a circle. Choose one person to be "it." "It" then must go over and sit on someone's lap (guy or girl) and say, "Darling, I love you, will you smile for me?" The person must reply, "I love you, honey, but I cannot smile for you." The person replying must keep a straight face while saying his/her lines. If "it" can get the "victim" to laugh, the "victim" becomes "it" and the game continues. Play as long as you like or until everyone is laughing so hard that they can't talk.

MUSICAL CANDY
Have everyone sit in a circle. Play some music and pass a full box of Valentine's candy around the group. When the music stops, whoever is holding the box may choose a piece and eat it. Continue the game until the candy is gone or until everyone has had at least one piece. (If someone is on a diet, or can't have chocolate, give them the option of kissing one of the people sitting around the circle instead of eating a piece of candy.)

FREE KISSES
Before the group comes, put up signs saying, "This way to kissing room. Test your pucker power." etc. Then, on the door of a room, place other signs that say: "Rate your kiss here! Enter at your own risk. Prizes awarded to the best kisser," etc. Assign two people to be inside the room. When a person enters the room, have him close the door. Then have the couple bring out a tray of candy kisses and offer the person one. He/she should be told to keep the secret of the game after he leaves and maybe even "talk it up a bit." If you think your group will be reluctant to give it a try, clue someone in on the plan to get the action going.

GREAT PAIRS AND LOVERS

Write each name of a famous pair on a slip of paper and mix them up. As each person joins the party, pin a name on his back. Each then must ask "Yes, No" questions of the people in the room to find out who his is. Once everyone discovers who he is he must find his mate. When everyone is paired off, try the game "Hearts in Hand."

Some famous pairs are: Romeo and Juliet, The Captain and Tennille, Donny and Marie Osmond, Mark Antony and Cleopatra, Pocahontas and Captain John Smith, Donald Duck and Daisy, Charlie Brown and Peppermint Patty, Lil' Abner and Daisy Mae, Elton John and Olivia Newton John, Jimmy and Roselyn Carter, Pierre and Margaret Trudeau, Samson and Delilah, Adam and Eve, Mickey and Minnie Mouse.

HEARTS IN HAND

Have the group pair off teams with one guy and one girl on each team. Place a telephone book or a Sears catalogue on the floor (any large, thick book will do). Scatter about 50-75 candy hearts all around the book so they are within possible reach. As the couple both stand on the book, the girl must stoop down, pick up a candy heart and hand it up to the guy. If they lose their balance and a foot touches the floor, the couple is disqualified. The couple who picks up the most hearts in sixty seconds wins.

HALLOWEEN

BROOMSTICK RELAY

In a large room divide the group into two teams and give each team a broom. For each team place three boxes in a row several yards apart.

In box #1 place a Halloween mask and the directions: "Hold the mask to your face and scream, 'Anything for Halloween.'" (Adapt the saying to whatever is said in your area.)

In box #2 place a witch's hat and the directions: "Put the witch's hat on and in a cackly, witchy voice say, 'Bubble, bubble, toil and trouble.'" (Adapt the saying to whatever you think a witch would say. The one above is from Shakespeare's Macbeth.)

In box #3 place a half moon shape and the directions: "Hold the moon high over your head and howl like a werewolf."

You may add more boxes and ideas if you like.

Each group member must place the broom between his legs and "ride" the broom to each box; then he must follow the directions and continue on to the next box. When all three "feats" are accomplished, he must ride the broom back and pass it to the next person in line. The first team finished wins.

Be sure that the broom is touching the floor as the person rides it.

FIND IT IF YOU CAN

Have a scavenger hunt but have the items related to the theme of Halloween. Some of the items can be silly to force the group to use their imagination; others can be ordinary. Examples:

    a witch's eye (this could be a marble)
    a bat's wing (this could be a chicken wing)
    four pieces of "chicken corn" candy
    a pumpkin no larger than 12" in diameter
    an old doorbell stuck with ten straight pins
    two feet of black streamers
    a popped orange balloon
    twelve grains of Indian corn
    a dozen pumpkin seeds

WITCH HUNT

Cut out twenty-five or more pieces of black cardboard in the shape of witches. Hide the pieces both inside and outside the building before or shortly after everyone has arrived. Pair off or go out individually to hunt for witches. The person to return with the most witches wins. Make sure each person or couple has a flashlight.

PUMPKIN PIE MAKERS

Instead of a scavenger hunt, go on a pumpkin pie making mission. Divide into groups of four or five. Give each group a pie plate, a recipe for making a pumpkin pie, and a few empty cans and bags to hold the collected ingredients. Have them go around from door to door asking for ONE of the ingredients listed. (If the recipe requires three eggs, they should go to three houses.) It's optional to make and bake the pies when you return.

Play It Like It Is

A simulation game is a special kind of game that acts as a "model" or a "simulation" of real life. It's a relatively new idea and although many of these games are very easy to play, they usually take about an hour and a half to complete. The biggest advantage of working with a simulation game is that in reflecting the real world process, it causes the participants to think about a certain situation, find out how they really feel, and later discuss what they've learned through the experience.

When you play a simulation game be sure to keep these points in mind.

1. These games are not designed for winning or losing — that's not their purpose. Everyone who participates wins. The cooperative-competition aspect of most real life situations is built into the games and winning is usually only a relative thing.
2. Most of these games do NOT require skillful role playing.
3. Playing the game is the most important aspect of the game since it is part of the learning experience.
4. Since these games are programmed as real life simulations, they will create real life tensions, frustrations, and feelings. Don't try to avoid these; they are part of the learning experience.
5. Stop the game when you feel that most of the learning has already taken place. Don't let the game drag on or it will hinder the good effects.
6. The most important part of the game comes when it is finished and it's time to sit and discuss what happened. Hopefully the discussion will start spontaneously and the leader will only act as a guide. Just in case, have a set of prepared questions, but use them only if spontaneous discussion fails.

When you feel the discussion has climaxed, stop. It's better to have the group go home with the experience fresh in their minds than to lecture them out of what they learned. Going home with unhappy feelings means they have had an unhappy experience, regardless of how the actual game went.

$20,000 DECISION

INTRODUCTION

$20,000 is a lot of money. Every church can put that kind of money to good use and the Church of the Good Samaritan is no exception. An anonymous donor has left the church $20,000 with the following requirement attached: all the money must be used for one project only. If the church committees cannot agree upon a project, they must return the money.

The Church of the Good Samaritan has a problem. It has four very strong interest groups in the church and each wants to use the money. The committees include:
1. The Youth Center Committee — they want to establish a community youth center.
2. The Educational Committee — they want to expand the education program of the church: Sunday School, catechism, young people's, etc.
3. The Missions Committee — they want to establish another foreign mission station.
4. The Building Committee — they want to remodel and air-condition the church.

The object of the game is for one committee to secure a total of fifty-one votes (a majority) within six rounds, and to have the votes ratified by the council so they will get the money.

PARTICIPANTS

— A game leader who directs the game.
— A pastor who leads the council meetings and mediates the discussion between the various groups. Five votes of influence.
— Committees: the remaining people are divided equally into the following four groups.
  1. The Youth Center Committee; ten votes of influence.
  2. The Educational Committee; fifteen votes of influence.
  3. The Mission Committee; fifteen votes of influence.
  4. The Building Committee; twenty votes of influence.
— The Council which is made up of two elected members from each committee and the pastor. They only meet when the pastor calls them, but they must meet after the last (sixth) round.
— A Negotiator who is elected by each committee to talk with the other committees about their decision.
— The Chairman of each committee who is responsible for his committee's actions.

MATERIALS NEEDED

100 playing chips
Dice
A large score sheet which looks like this:

Round Number	Start	1	2	3	4	5	6	Final
Youth Center Committee								
Education Committee								
Mission Committee								
Building Committee								

The following "Decision Cards":

You had an effective fund raising.
EARN 3 POINTS

The Youth Center Committee behaved poorly at a recent congregational meeting.
TAKE 3 POINTS FROM THE YOUTH CENTER COMMITTEE

Your attitudes were definitely un-Christian the last time you tried to "bargain."
LOSE 3 POINTS

FOR EDUCATION COMMITTEE ONLY:
Sunday School attendance is down.
LOSE 3 POINTS

For the next round throw your support to the other committees. The following round you will again have the same support as before.

FOR YOUTH COMMITTEE ONLY:
You used underhanded tactics and tried to subvert the needs of the other committees.
LOSE 5 POINTS

FOR BUILDING COMMITTEE ONLY:
You placed material things above human needs.
GIVE 2 POINTS TO EACH COMMITTEE

You insulted the Council.
LOSE 2 POINTS

Your cause was publicized in the denominational magazine.
EARN 5 POINTS

Your chairman was rude to the Youth Center Committee.
GIVE 3 POINTS TO THE YOUTH CENTER COMMITTEE

FOR BUILDING COMMITTEE ONLY:
The other committees will lose the support of the influential members of the church if you don't help.
TAKE 2 POINTS FROM EACH COMMITTEE

FOR EDUCATION COMMITTEE ONLY:
Fifteen young people made profession of faith as a result of catechism.
EARN 3 POINTS

FOR MISSION COMMITTEE ONLY:
You failed to keep the needs of the Foreign Missions Board before the congregation.
LOSE 3 POINTS

FOR YOUTH CENTER COMMITTEE ONLY:
You persuaded the parents of the Church's youth group to support your cause.
EARN 5 POINTS

You have earned the support of the minister for this round ONLY.
TAKE 5 POINTS

Your committee is unable to reach a unanimous decision.
LOSE 2 POINTS

You exceeded your negotiating period.
LOSE 2 POINTS

Your canvassing methods are great.
DOUBLE YOUR EARNINGS THE NEXT TIME YOU THROW

You may not initiate any more negotiating for the rest of the game — you must wait for others to approach you.

You have insulted the Pastor.
LOSE 1 TURN

Give your next card to another group or keep it, but you must decide before looking at it.

FOR MISSION COMMITTEE ONLY:
You received a letter indicating the need for additional missionaries on the foreign mission field.
EARN 3 POINTS

RULES

1. Votes
   a. Each group starts with a certain number of votes (see list above).
   b. The pastor also has 5 votes.
   c. The other 35 votes, represented by chips, belong to uncommitted members of the congregation.
   d. Votes can be earned or lost through negotiations, council decisions, opportunity cards, or penalty cards.
2. Each round lasts 8-10 minutes.
3. If all the chips are out on the floor, no additional chips may be given out until some have been returned.
4. Committees may negotiate and may pool chips, loan them for one period or more, or give them permanently to another group.
5. In times of hostility, the pastor is responsible for smoothing the rough edges.
6. The council may meet at any time to impose new rules, make adjustments, or punish committees or chairmen. The council runs by majority vote. The pastor does not vote, except in the case of a tie.
7. The game continues for 6 rounds, or about an hour.

PLAYING

1. The chairman of each committee throws 2 dice at the beginning of each round. With the total he may either choose the points or do the following.

If he throws a:	He receives:
2 or 12	4 chips
3 or 11	3 chips
4 or 10	2 chips
5 or 9	1 chip
6, 7, or 8	1 decision card

2. Following the above procedure the groups are free to negotiate until the 10 minutes are up.
3. When time is up, each team chairman must report the total number of chips they now have to the pastor.
4. If any team has over 51 chips, a council meeting is called. The council must make a decision to "accept" this as the congregation's decision or they may decide to subtract or distribute some of these chips to other committees. They may do whatever they like.

DISCUSSION IDEAS

1. Discuss the relative importance of the four areas involved: missions, youth, education, and building.
2. Discuss the interaction between the committees and relate this to the way groups work and the way a church functions.
3. Discuss group dynamics, leadership, tension, and tension relief.

SHOPPING OR SHOPLIFTING

This game simulates the real life pressures on businessmen and the temptation and techniques of those who steal. This is an easy game to play in about an hour and a half (including discussion time).

PREPARATION

1. In a square place a number of chairs so that there are six less chairs than players (E.g. if you have 26 people, use only 20 chairs).
2. Give each chair a different number.
3. Each chair represents one store. You may want to label each chair as a specific store: furniture, appliance, hardware, etc. Have appropriate items for each.
4. Fold about 20 or more (the exact number will depend on the number in your group) 3 x 5 cards in half. On the outside of the card write the name of an article you can buy: radio, CB, hairdryer, coat, etc. On the inside write a number to represent "points." The number should reflect the "value" of the item. Staple the cards shut.
5. Place 3 cards on each chair.
6. On another set of 3 x 5 cards write the numbers that appear on the chairs. On 2 other 3 x 5 cards write "detective." On 4 other 3 x 5 cards write "thief." (You should now have 1 - 3 x 5 card for each player.)
7. Place 1 of the above cards (either marked with a number or "thief" or "detective" plus 3 poker chips ("money") into an envelope. Seal the envelope.
8. Give each person in the group an envelope. Those who receive a card with a number on it become the shopkeeper of the "store" with the same number. Those who receive a word must play "detective" or "thief" as indicated.

PLAYING

1. When the game begins the detectives must be on the lookout for the thieves. If they spot one, they simply tap him on the left shoulder and lead him into another room. The thief is now out of the game. If anyone impersonates a detective, he automatically loses the game.
2. Although each of the cards has a number of points on it, collecting points is not the object of the game. But let the players think that points *are* important.
3. Tell the group that the object of the game is to shop around and continue to keep six objects: either cards and/or chips.
4. If and when a shop owner finds something missing from his store, he must replace the item by stealing from another shop. He cannot report it to the detectives, since he does not know who the detectives are.
5. Each person should keep his identity secret. Shop owners should move around and leave their stores. If their identity is discovered, they are out of the game.
6. If the identity of anyone except the detectives is revealed, they are out of the game. But the detectives should try to remain secret in order to catch more thieves, including shopkeepers who may steal from one another.

7. Shopping is done by merely picking up a card and placing the chip down in its place. All chips and cards on the chair remain the property of the shop owner.
8. Scoring:
A shopkeeper receives one point for every card and chip he has in his hand and/or in his store. Thieves receive one point for every chip they have minus the three they started with in their envelope. Thieves may not steal after they have been caught. Their points remain good, however. The detectives receive three points for every thief they catch. Chips have no value for detectives; they are only used to hide their identity.
9. When the points are counted, everyone having six or more points is a winner. Those with less are considered losers.

DISCUSSION QUESTIONS

1. What was the feeling you had knowing that some people were stealing?
2. Were you suspicious of everyone?
3. Did you favor and trust your friends more or less?
4. Did you receive any comfort from the fact that there were two detectives?
5. Did you as a shopkeeper or thief go after the higher point items? Why?
6. How did you feel when you were robbed?
7. Did you feel pressured to rob someone else?
8. Were the two detectives suspicious about everyone?
9. Were you falsely arrested during the game? How did you feel about not having a trial?
10. How is this game like real life?
11. What does the Bible have to say about these subjects?

— adapted from SIMULATION GAMES FOR RELIGIOUS EDUCATION

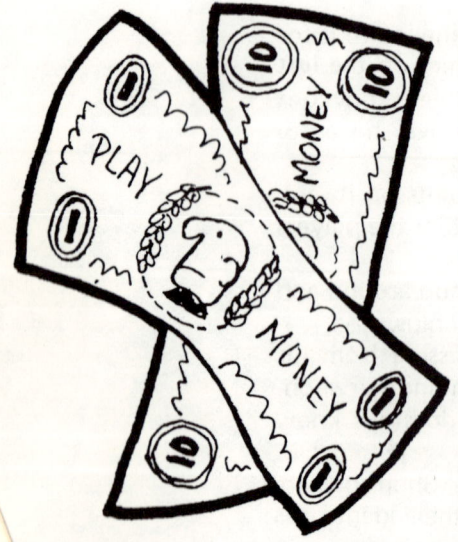

BLACK-RED GAME

This is a simulation game emphasizing competition and trust. Divide the group into two teams. You'll need some play money and a copy of the chart below. Give each team $50. Tell them that they will each be given ten opportunities to choose either red or black. Then explain the results included in the chart below. Tell them that the object of the game is to double their own money (NOT to get more money than the other team). Take each choice separately and announce the results before proceeding to the next opportunity. Groups work best in separate rooms. After rounds four and seven ask one group if they wish to negotiate with the other group. Continue the game for the ten rounds. Have a discussion following the game on trust, greed, fear, cooperation, competition, selfishness, poverty, or any subject which could possibly relate to this game.

		If room 1 chooses	
		RED	BLACK
If room 2 chooses	RED	Both teams lose five dollars	Team 1 loses $10 Team 2 wins $10
	BLACK	Team 1 wins $10 Team 2 loses $10	Both teams win five dollars

COMMUNITY DISASTER

The leader gives each player a role in a simulated community. When the game begins, the leader informs players that a disaster has occurred in some part of town. The player must find out where the disaster has occurred, if any of his friends or relatives have been hurt or killed, and maintain his function in the community to facilitate aid to the disaster area. Confusion results which must be changed into "togetherness" in order to aid disaster relief. This game is best played by about 10 people.

Write to John Hopkins University, Department of Social Relations, Charles and 34th Streets, Baltimore, MD 21218.

450 BLESSINGS

This simulation game takes you back to the time of the Protestant reformation and the struggle of the Anabaptists, but it's easily adaptable for our situation today. It deals with the persecution of Christians. The goal of the game is to acquire 450 blessings by memorizing scripture verses. In going through life, however, persecutions set in and blessings are taken away. A player who is not careful may end up excommunicated or in jail. This game is created for small groups and lasts 45 minutes to an hour. It could be adapted for groups up to a dozen.

Available in the October, 1975 issue of *"With"* magazine. Write to *With*, 616 Walnut Avenue, Scottdale, PA 15683. Please enclose $1.00.

THE GAME OF LIFE

This game tries to simulate real life. Jobs, salaries, expenses of owning a home, some chance, the church and local government are all included in the game plan. The participants must go through the daily routine of life. The game even has its boring moments — typical of life. The game takes about an hour and a half and is excellent for any group size above 12.

Available for 95¢ from CSS, 628 S. Main Street, Lima, OH 45804.

THE JAIL PUZZLE

This excellent game is about justice, criminals, and our court system. The game involves 12 to 40 people who find themselves in actual society with all of the frustrations and anxiety of criminals, jail guards, and judges. The game takes about 1 1/2 to 2 hours and is excellent in developing a group feeling as well as learning something about justice in our society.

Rules and game plans are available from Sam E. De Bose, 616 North Highland Avenue, Pittsburgh, PA 15206. Please enclose $1.00 for postage and expense.

PARENT-CHILD GAME

This game simulates the frustrations and responsibilities of family life centered around the adolescent's behavior. The group is divided into pairs who must continually interact for points. The teenager wins points by coming to an agreement with his parent; the parent wins points by getting the teenager to comply with his wishes. The adolescent and the parent with the most points win the game.

A complete set of rules is available from John Hopkins University, Department of Social Relations, Charles and 34th Streets, Baltimore, MD 21218.

THE POVERTY GAME

Poverty is obviously no game! This simulation game is designed for the purpose of experiencing poverty and community interaction. The participants are divided into 13 groups. Each is assigned to a sub-section of a community known as "Clusteropolis," ranging from the "town council" to a "militant poor people's group." If you have a group of mature young people or young adults who really want a learning experience, this is an excellent game. Allow three hours to benefit the most from this game.

Available free from the Lutheran Church in America, Youth Ministry Cluster #60, R.D.#1, Box 349-C, Mt. Wolf, PA 17347.

REAL WORLD GAME

In the world today starvation is a reality. Many countries cannot grow enough food to feed their people. This game, designed for large groups of 28 to 70, simulates that hunger situation by dividing all the players into seven groups, each representing one country. Through monthly production and income, each nation must beg, borrow, or steal enough food for their people. There are some countries with plenty to spare, some with great needs. The game is excellent for developing community spirit and an interest in the food crisis. Allow 2 hours for playing.

This game is found in the book *Far-Out Ideas* by Wayne Rice and Mike Yaconelli, Zondervan Publishing, 1415 Lake Drive, SE, Grand Rapids, MI 49506. $2.95.